OSPREY NEW VANGUARD SERIES: 30

AMTRACS: US AMPHIBIOUS ASSAULT VEHICLES

WRITTEN BY STEVEN ZALOGA

COLOUR PLATES BY TERRY HADLER AND MIKE BADROCKE

OSPREY
MILITARY

First published in Great Britain in 1999 by Osprey Publishing,
Elms Court, Chapel Way, Botley, Oxford OX2 9LP
Email: osprey@osprey-publishing.co.uk

ISBN 1 85532 850 X

Editor: Nikolai Bogdanovic
Design: **Chris @ D4Design**

Origination by Valhaven Ltd, Isleworth, UK
Printed through World Print Ltd., Hong Kong

99 00 01 02 03   10 9 8 7 6 5 4 3 2 1

FOR A CATALOGUE OF ALL BOOKS PUBLISHED BY OSPREY MILITARY,
AUTOMOTIVE AND AVIATION PLEASE WRITE TO:

**The Marketing Manager, Osprey Direct UK, P.O. Box 140,
Wellingborough, Northants, NN8 4ZA, United Kingdom**

**The Marketing Manager, Osprey Direct USA, P.O. Box 130,
Sterling Heights, MI 48311-0130, USA**

VISIT OSPREY'S WEBSITE AT:
http://www.osprey-publishing.co.uk

Artist's note

Readers may care to note that the original centre cutaway painting from this
book is available for private sale. All reproduction copyright whatsoever is
retained by the Publishers. All enquiries should be addressed to:

Mike Badrocke, 37 Prospect Road, Southborough, Tunbridge Wells, Kent,
TN4 0EN

The Publishers regret that they can enter into no correspondence upon this
matter.

Author's note

The author would like to acknowledge the assistance of several friends whose
aid made this book possible. Thanks go to Jim Loop for material on US Army
amtracs, to Mike Green for his help in locating photos in the FMC archive, to
Norman Friedman for his help with US Navy production figures, and to Simon
Dunstan, Joe Bermudez, Bill Auerbach and George Balin for help in locating
photos.

TITLE PAGE **An LVT(A)-4 of the Marine 3rd Armored
Amphibian Battalion on the beach at Peleliu,
15 September 1944.**

AMTRACS: US AMPHIBIOUS ASSAULT VEHICLES

AMPHIBIAN VEHICLES

Few military operations are as difficult and risky as an amphibious landing against a contested beachhead, as was all too evident in Britain's ill-fated Gallipoli landings in World War I. In the 1920s and 1930s, US Marine planners contemplated new solutions to this age-old tactical problem. Not surprisingly, the main focus of new equipment programmes was on the development of modern landing boats. This quickly exhausted the meagre funding available and prevented much experimentation with tracked landing craft.

The imaginative and irascible American inventor, J. Walter Christie, proposed amphibious tracked vehicles to both the US Army and the US Marine Corps in the early 1920s. He offered his M.1923 amphibious tank to the Marine Corps for trials, and it was used experimentally during the 1924 amphibious exercise at Culebra, Puerto Rico. The M.1923 amphibian could better be described as a self-propelled gun, as its 75mm gun was not turret-mounted, but fitted in the hull. The Marine Corps, while finding the concept interesting, felt that the Christie

Roebling's original Alligator, completed in 1935, bore little resemblance to the later amtracs. It proved to be too slow and too heavy, as well as unmanageable in water. (FMC Corp.)

amphibian was unsea-worthy and unsatisfactory in other respects, and decided against adopting it. Instead, the Marine Corps adopted the Six-Ton Special Tractor (the US-built version of the French Renault FT light tank), which was small enough to be landed from lighters or barges for amphibious operations. The Marines were convinced of the value of armoured vehicles in supporting beach landings, but in the 1930s lacked sufficient funding for much ex-perimentation with armoured or amphibious vehicles.

The second model of the Alligator, completed in 1937, attracted US Marine Corps attention and led to the LVT-1. (FMC Corp.)

In 1937, an article appeared in *Life* magazine of a tracked amphibious vehicle, the Alligator, which had been developed for rescue operations in the swamps of Florida. This attracted Marine Corps attention; and after inspection of the vehicle, the Navy was asked to secure pilot models for trials, and possible acquisition.

The Alligator was the result of private efforts by members of one of America's most illustrious engineering families, the Roeblings. John and Donald Roebling, the son and grandson of Col. Washington Roebling (builder of the Brooklyn Bridge) had built the vehicle, using their own funds, after witnessing the disastrous results of several hurricanes in the swampy Okeechobee region of Florida. Donald Roebling attempted to develop a vehicle which would bridge the gap between 'where a boat grounded and a car flooded out'. The Alligator was intended to serve as a rescue vehicle in swampy areas that were inaccessible to either boats or vehicles: he used aluminium construction to save on weight, and an unusual track suspension that provided propulsion both in the water and on land. The first Alligator was completed in 1935 but its performance was disappointing, mainly because its water speed was a paltry 2.3 mph. A series of redesigns culminated in a virtually new vehicle by 1937. This model was shorter and wider than the original 1935 form but, more importantly, used a sturdier track and suspension system. It weighed 3,100lb less (8,700lb) and had a water speed of 8.6 mph; and it was this 1937 model that so impressed the Marine officers.

The Navy, however, was not so enthused, especially because of its clumsy performance at sea compared to conventional boats, so the Marine request was rejected on the grounds of economy. The Marines persisted; and in October 1939 Gen. Moses, the president of the Marines Equipment Board, convinced Roebling to design a vehicle specifically for military use. The new 1940 model, sometimes called the Crocodile, was lighter in weight and performed better than earlier models. Although it was not as manoeuvrable as a boat of comparable size, its pontoon design made it more seaworthy in rough surf conditions.

The outbreak of war in Europe led to the expansion of the US military budget. The US Navy Bureau of Ships finally succumbed to Marine pressure and contracted Roebling to build a second prototype with a more powerful 120hp Lincoln-Zephyr engine. It was completed and delivered to Quantico in November 1940, and was used in Fleet Exercises in January–February 1941, the results greatly impressing both Navy and Marine observers. The Navy felt, however, that the aluminium construction was not rugged enough for military service, preferring steel, and that the track design would not endure the abrasive effects of sand and salt water; Roebling was contracted to produce a revised version incorporating these changes. As Roebling did not have access to actual production facilities, he turned to the Food Machinery Corporation (FMC) who had fabricated parts for the early Alligators. This was the first tracked military vehicle project for FMC, which went on to produce more armoured vehicles than any other company in the United States.

The new vehicle was officially dubbed LVT (Landing Vehicle Tracked), in keeping with the Navy nomenclature system for landing craft. FMC was awarded an initial contract for 200 LVTs besides the two prototypes, and the first was completed in July 1941. The contract was later increased, for a total of 1,225 LVT-1, popularly known as Alligators.

The first Marine amphibian tractor (variously called amtrac, amtrak and amphtrac) unit, the Amphibian Tractor Detachment, was formed in May 1941 at Dunedin, Florida. This unit formed the nucleus for the later 1st Amphibian Tractor Battalion of the 1st Marine Division, which completed organisation in February 1942 shortly after the outbreak of the war in the Pacific. The early conception of amtrac operations envisioned using the Alligators solely as amphibious supply vehicles. The LVT-1 was made of mild steel with no armour value: it was used to bring supplies from ships off-shore, onto and beyond the beaches. The track system, even when improved, was still very susceptible to damage when used on hard ground, so there were no plans to use the amtracs for prolonged periods on land. Indeed the early amtracs only had a life expectancy of about 200 hours' running time due to the stresses on the engine, suspension and track.

The plans called for the deployment of a single amphibian tractor battalion with each Marine division, initially numbering 75 vehicles per battalion. The first use of amtracs in a combat theatre took place in August 1942, when the 1st and 2nd Amphibian Tractor battalions were used to provide logistical support at

The LVT-1 Alligator first entered service in the Solomon Islands in 1942 at Guadalcanal, and later at Bougainville and Rendova in 1943. As seen here during the Bougainville campaign, it was used solely in the supply rôle. (USMC)

Guadalcanal in the Solomon Islands. In November 1942, Alligators with the Fleet Marine Force were used to bring supplies ashore during the landings in French Morocco as part of Operation 'Torch'. Alligators were used in a similar rôle at Attu in the Aleutian Islands off Alaska in May 1943, at Shemya Island in the Aleutians in August 1943, and at Rendova in the Solomon Islands in September 1943. The new 3rd Amphibian Tractor Battalion was employed at Bougainville in the Northern Solomons in November 1943.

TARAWA: NEW TACTICS

By 1943 the amtracs had proved to be very useful vehicles in uncontested amphibious landings, but for troop landings against contested beaches more conventional craft like LCVPs were used. The utility of amtracs as assault vehicles to carry troops was first demonstrated at Tarawa, in November 1943.

In 1943 the switch in the focus of US efforts, from the large tropical islands of the south-western Pacific to the rocky little atolls of the central Pacific, called for a shift in amphibious tactics. The tiny atolls did not offer the option of uncontested landings as had previously been the case. Most of the islands large enough to be of military value had been fortified by the Japanese. Landings would have to take place directly against fortified Japanese positions if the islands were to be seized. In

The first use of amtracs in an assault rôle took place at Tarawa in November 1943. Here, one of the surviving LVT-1 Alligators is lodged against the coconut log sea-wall on Betio at Red Beach Three. The improvised armour plate added to the cab is clearly evident. (USMC)

The LVT-2 Water Buffalo saw its combat debut at Tarawa. This LVT-2 was hit and burned along the beach edge at Betio. It has improvised armour on the oab front. In the background are a sunken M4A2 Sherman tank, and a number of disabled amtracs. (USMC)

The Borg-Warner Model A was a parallel attempt to develop an improved amtrac alongside similar efforts by FMC. It was equipped with a turret from an M3A1 light tank, seen here pointed over the rear of the vehicle. The Model A and Model B later led to the LVT-3 Bushmaster. (US Navy)

addition, many of the islands in the atolls were ringed by coral reefs which were too shallow for Higgins boats like the LCVPs and LCMs in certain tidal conditions.

The first of these island fortresses to be attacked was Betio in the Tarawa atoll. Elements of the 2nd Marine Division were to seize Betio, while army units seized the less heavily defended island of Makin: Betio was surrounded by a coral reef of undetermined depth which greatly concerned Marine planners. The Navy was convinced that the reef was sufficiently submerged to permit a loaded Higgins boat to safely pass over it; the Marines were not. Maj. David M. Shoup, the 2nd Marine Division operations officer (and later one of the heroes of Tarawa), had served with the division on Guadalcanal and remembered the yeoman service provided by the amtracs of the 1st and 2nd Amphibian Tractor battalions. Shoup concluded that the amtracs would be ideal for the Betio landing, since they could readily surmount the fringing reef if it was indeed too shallow. The divisional commander, Gen. Julian Smith, presented his plans to the Marine commander of the ground elements of the amphibious force, Maj.Gen. Holland M. ('Howlin' Mad') Smith. Julian Smith convinced H.M. Smith of the need for the amtracs, as well as mentioning that the navy had little enthusiasm for the notion. H.M. Smith visited his navy counterpart for Operation 'Galvanic', R-Adm. Richmond Kelly Turner, to request more amtracs than the 100 worn-out LVT-1s of the 2nd Amphibian Tractor Battalion at Wellington, Australia. The cantankerous Turner echoed the navy's opposition to the use of amtracs, saying that the Higgins boats could clear the fringing reef and that the amtracs were unseaworthy. The major-general viewed the navy's attitude as callous indifference to the Marines rather than any serious objection to the novel use of amtracs. 'Howlin' Mad' Smith was as stubborn as Turner, and, after a bitter argument, concluded: 'No amtracs, no operation!' Turner relented and promised a further 100 new amtracs from the naval base at Somoa.

By the autumn of 1943 the 100 LVT-1 amtracs of the 2nd Amphibian Tractor Battalion had long since passed their theoretical life expectancy due to their use on Guadalcanal. Most had already chalked up over 400 hours of running time compared to their 200-hour average life expectancy, and only 75 could be salvaged. The corrosive effects of sea water on their suspension and propulsion, and their generally worn-out condition, were so severe that the unit was wary of any rehearsals for the landing which would further wear them down. Only 50 of the new LVT-2s were delivered before the operation.

The LVT-2 Water Buffalo

The LVT-2 had been developed to overcome shortcomings in the initial LVT-1 design.

Development began in 1941 by the Bureau of Ships and FMC. The LVT-2 used a new torsilastic sprung suspension which offered a better ride on land as well as greater durability. The powertrain was taken directly from the M3A1 light tank, and provided greater power and reliability. The LVT-2 (also called LVT Mk. II or Water Buffalo) was first ordered into production in June 1942, but did not reach combat units until 1943. It had a life expectancy three times as high as the LVT-1 (600 vs. 200 running hours); but the tracks had to be replaced every 150 hours or so, especially if run over hard terrain.

The commander of the 2nd Amphibian Tractor Battalion, Maj. Henry Drewes, was told by Gen. Julian Smith that his amtracs could expect to encounter very heavy fire in spite of Navy promises to 'obliterate' the Japanese defences on Betio, and suggested that Drewes add armour plating to the amtracs. Drewes searched Wellington for armour, and finally found some rusted 9mm plate outside the city, which was cut and prepared by the General Motors plant in Wellington and attached to the LVT-1s. The few officers who survived the assault felt that the armour saved many lives; many of the crews argued otherwise, but nearly all agreed that it was an important morale booster. In addition, machine-gun mounts were added to the amtracs; usually a .50-cal. in front, and two .30-cal. machine-guns on the side or rear.

The shortage of amtracs for Operation 'Galvanic' inevitably meant that only a proportion of the troops were landed using them: the first three waves would be carried in on the amtracs, followed by reinforcements in LCVPs (Higgins boats). The first wave used 42 of the available 125 amtracs. The attack on Betio Island on 20 November 1943 was preceded by a fearsome naval and air bombardment, totalling some

LVT(A)-1s of the Army 708th Amphibian Tank Battalion come ashore at Saipan on D-Day, 15 June 1944. Neither the Army nor the Marines were completely happy with the LVT(A)-1 due to the small gun carried, but it continued in service through the end of the war. Note the rear machine-gun tubs. (USMC)

3,000 tons of munitions onto an island only 291 acres in area. Nevertheless, the Japanese forces had ample time to fortify the island, and the commander had boasted that it would take 'a million men, a hundred years' to capture the island from his crack Special Naval Landing Forces (Japanese marines).

The durability of the Japanese bunkers became all too clear as the amtracs of the first wave approached the beach at a turtle crawl. They surmounted the fringing reef without difficulty, but came under an intense barrage from heavy machine-guns, mortars and artillery from the surviving bunkers. Eight of the amtracs were sunk on the approach, and many more suffered so much damage from bullets and shrapnel that they later sank when attempting to return to sea for reloading. The added armour offered modest protection against small-arms fire, but was inadequate against heavy machine-gun fire. The machine-gunners on board were particularly hard hit, since their weapons were largely unprotected and they had to expose themselves to fire them. By the end of the operation only 35 amtracs were still operational. A total of 52 LVT-1s and 30 LVT-2s had been lost to enemy action, and eight to mechanical failures. Of these, 35 had been sunk directly by gunfire; 26 were disabled by gunfire and shrapnel after having surmounted the reef, nine had burned on the beach after their fuel tanks were hit; and two were blown up by mines. Of the 500 amtrac crewmen, 323 were killed or wounded, including the battalion commander Maj. Drewes, killed by gunfire while commanding the first wave.

In spite of the losses, the amtracs had managed to deliver a significant number of troops to the beachhead successfully. The same was not true of the Higgins boats in the fourth, fifth and sixth waves. As

A pair of LVT(A)-1s of the Marine 1st Armored Amphibian Battalion in action in the Marshalls in the summer of 1944. There was some controversy over the use of amtracs, and whether they should conduct their fire support missions while in the water off-shore, as seen here, or on the beach itself. (USMC)

the Marine planners had feared, they failed to clear the fringing reefs, and the marines inside were obliged to disembark and wade ashore from distances of 300 to 800 yards under intense Japanese machine-gun fire. It was a slaughter, with single Japanese machine-guns killing or wounding entire boat-loads of marines.

To support the beachhead, a dozen M4A2 Sherman tanks of the 1st Marine Amphibious Corps Tank Battalion were brought up on LCM landing craft. As with the troops, the tank landing craft were stopped by the fringing reef. Only three tanks eventually made their way safely to the beach, most being lost in the water due to engine flooding, or sinking into the gaping shell craters caused by naval gunfire. While the tanks were later to prove invaluable in the capture of the island, their early difficulties reaching the beach highlighted the need for immediate fire support during the initial assault phase, preferably in the form of some sort of amphibious tank.

After 76 hours of bloody fighting, Betio was taken. The costs were staggering: 3,400 Marine casualties, a third of these killed; and virtually the entire garrison of 2,600 Japanese SNLF marines. The nightmarish image of the slaughter of the marines wading ashore from the beached Higgins boats led to USMC insistence on the use of amtracs to carry out any amphibious landings against contested beaches in the future. The Marine Corps had concluded that amtracs had made the critical difference between victory and defeat at Tarawa. If all the landings had been conducted using the LCVPs and LCMs, the landing would probably have been a very bloody failure. The heavy cost of the battle caused a scandal back in the United States. The Marines had no difficulty over their request for expanded production of amtracs, and the Navy's reluctance to use amtracs in amphibious landings evaporated. The US Army, responsible for amphibious operations in the South-West Pacific, paid careful attention to the lessons of Tarawa, and began expanding its own amtrac units.

At Tinian, a coral cliff would have prevented the amtracs from advancing beyond the beach, leading to the development of the Doodlebug, seen here. This LVT-2 had a special timber ramp to surmount the obstacle, and six of these were used during the Tinian landing. (USMC)

AMTANKS AND FIRE SUPPORT

In 1941, during the development of the LVT-2, the design teams were asked to investigate the possibility of developing an armed and armoured version of the new amtrac. This took place before the Tarawa landings, and the requirement appears to have been based on concerns that amphibious landings might face Japanese tank units. Steel armour of between 6mm and 12mm was employed in place of the sheet steel used on the normal LVT-2. The M6 37mm tank gun was the largest anti-tank weapon that could be adopted due to weight and recoil restrictions. The turret was adapted from the M5A1 Stuart light tank turret, and was identical except for the deletion of the rear turret radio bustle. Two .30-cal. machine-guns were added on scarf rings behind the turret to provide additional fire support. The armour and turret added about three tons to the weight of the vehicle, but this did not seriously degrade vehicle buoyancy since no troops or supplies were to be carried. The new vehicle, the LVT(A)-1, was type classified and entered production in December 1943, a month after the Tarawa landing. These vehicles were usually called amtanks (or amphtanks) to distinguish them from the amtracs. During the development of the LVT(A)-1, the US Army placed a requirement for an armoured amtrac. This was developed concurrently with the LVT(A)-1, as the T33. It was a cross between the LVT-2 and the LVT(A)-1, having the armoured hull and cab of the LVT(A)-1 and the general storage configuration of the LVT-2. It entered production in 1943 for the US Army as the LVT(A)-2.

The Tarawa experience also prompted the US Army to accelerate development of amphibious versions of normal tanks. This took two directions: the development of improved wading gear for tanks dropped into shallow water, and the development of detachable pontoons and propulsion systems to enable tanks to swim ashore from some distance. Various types of wading gear were widely used in amphibious landings by both M4 Sherman and M5A1 Stuart tanks. The pontoon systems, such as M19 (Ritchie T-6) Swimming Device fitted to M4 medium tanks, were not ready in significant numbers until the last major operation of the war on Okinawa, where 20 Marine Shermans were landed by means of these systems. The DD tanks (Duplex Drive), developed in Britain for the Normandy invasion, were used by US tank battalions in Europe, but they never made an appearance in the Pacific. There was very little interplay between the two theatres in terms of specialised equipment development. Likewise, the applicability of LVTs for the Normandy

The Army's 2nd Engineer Special Brigade Support Battery modified some LVT(A)-2s into fire support vehicles, like this one seen here firing into Japanese dug-outs on Schouten Island in the Netherlands Indies in 1944. Barrage rocket projectors were mounted in the cargo bay, and a 37mm aircraft gun (from the P-39 fighter) was mounted on the rear. (US Army)

invasion was brushed aside as being unnecessary. The US infantry at Omaha Beach would be forced to relearn Tarawa's bloody lesson of the vulnerability of unprotected infantry wading ashore from landing craft.

The late production models of the LVT-2 built after March 1944 had an armoured cab and protected rear air intakes. This version is very difficult to distinguish from the Army LVT(A)-2, which also had integral hull and bow armour. This is a Marine LVT-2 on Iwo Jima, with added gun shields. (USMC)

Amtrac organisation

Under the E-Series Table of Organisation and Equipment (TOE) of April 1943, each Marine Division had an organic Amphibian Tractor Battalion, with too amtracs organised into three companies. The USMC eventually raised 11 amphibian tractor battalions plus a number of smaller detachments. In the spring of 1944, between the Kwajalein and Saipan operations, the amphibian tractor battalions were removed from divisional control, and retained at corps level for better co-ordination during landing operations. In October 1943, the USMC and the US Army began raising their first amtank battalions, the US Army christening them Amphibian Tank Battalions, while the Marines called their units Armored Amphibian Battalions. The Marine amtank battalions had four companies of 18 LVT(A)-1s, totalling 72, plus three LVT-2s in battalion HQ; while the Army battalions initially had four companies of 17 LVT(A)-1s, plus four LVT(A)-2 amtracs in battalion HQ. The Army battalion TOE was later enlarged to 18 amtanks and two amtracs per company, with battalion strength rising to 75 LVT(A) amtanks and 12 LVT amtracs.

The first US Army amphibian tractor battalions were raised concurrently with the new amtank battalions. The Army's bureaucracy had been sceptical of the amtracs after early tests in 1942, finding them very clumsy to operate. However, US Army units in the Pacific recognised their utility in the swampy conditions of the South-West Pacific, even if only for logistical support, and had been requesting amtracs for some time. Priority of amtrac deliveries went to the Marines, however, and the first US Army amtracs did not appear in the Pacific until early 1944. The first two amtank and two amtrac battalions were raised at the Army's Amphibious Training Center at Ft. Ord, California, on 27 October 1943 on the basis of existing armoured infantry and tank units. The US Army amphibian tractor battalions were organised slightly differently from their Marine counterparts: there were two companies, each with 51 amtracs, and a total of 119 amtracs per battalion. Although the amtrac is more closely associated with the US Marine Corps, it is worth noting that the US Army actually formed more amphibian battalions during the war than the Marines: seven Army and three Marine amtank battalions; and 23 Army and 11 Marine amtrac battalions. Likewise, 55 per cent of all amtracs went to the Army, and only 40 per cent to the Marines.

Debut of the amtank

The Marine 1st Amphibian Tractor Battalion was used to provide logistical support during the operations at Arawe and Cape Gloucester on New Britain in December 1943. The next major assault landing since Tarawa was scheduled for the Marshalls in February 1944, with both Army and Marine amphibian battalions participating. Kwajalein is the longest atoll in the world, stretching some 60 miles with a 20-mile-wide lagoon, and ideally suited to amtrac operations. US planners feared another Tarawa, and so prepared to make extensive use of tanks and amtanks. Army troops were assigned to Kwajalein and a number of smaller islands in the atoll, using the Provisional Amphibian Tractor Battalion supported by the Marines' new 1st Armored Amphibian Battalion. The Provisional Amphibian Tractor Battalion had been formed around the Army's premier amtank battalion, the 708th Amphibian Tank Battalion. However, the battalion had not received sufficient LVT(A)-1s, and so was reorganised in an improvised fashion with LVT(A)-1s, LVT(A)-2s and LVT-2s. This operation marked the combat debut of the LVT(A)-1 in both Army and Marine service. The Marine 4th Amphibian Tractor Battalion was split to form two additional battalions, the 10th and 11th Amphibian Tractor battalions, causing

The new LVT-3 Bushmasters were first used in combat on Okinawa where they were used to land troops of the 6th Marine Division. These Bushmasters have the optional armour kit fitted on the bow. (USMC)

significant problems in the conduct of the landings in the Marshalls as the units had so little time for training.

Usual Marine tactics for amtank deployment were to position an amtank company in line in front of each wave of amtracs. Usually, naval gunfire was restricted from firing too close to the landing beach, so the gunfire of the amtanks covered this gap. The 17 or 18 LVT(A)-1s proceeded in the lead to the beach and, when in range, began to open fire with their 37mm guns and three .30-cal. machine-guns. The intention was to force the Japanese defenders to keep their heads down with suppressive fire, rather than to pick off particular targets. There was some controversy during the initial operations regarding the final approach to the beach. The initial doctrine developed by the amtank battalions was that the amtanks would reach shallow water, then echelon off to the flank to allow the amtracs to proceed to the beach. They would maintain their position off the coast, in hull defilade in the water, providing covering fire until tanks could be landed in subsequent waves. The aim was to keep the amtanks in the water where they would be less vulnerable to enemy anti-tank guns: on land the LTV(A)-1 was like a beached whale, and its thin armour offered no protection against heavy machine-gun fire or anti-tank guns. On the other hand, the Marine infantry commanders wanted the amtanks up on the beaches so that they could co-ordinate their fire support with local units until the tanks arrived. The Marine amtank crews objected to many of the infantry requests, feeling that the infantry officers needlessly exposed their fragile vehicles to hostile fire in rôles better suited to normal tanks. Many of the infantry officers simply didn't understand how thinly armoured

Although the amtank battalions had suggested that the LVT(A)-1 be withdrawn from service due to its shortcomings, it was used right through the Okinawa campaign, as in the case of these late-model LVT(A)-1s near Chatan on D-Day, 1 April 1945. The late-model LVT(A)-1s had protected engine grills, a bow machine-gun, and additional armour around the rear machine-gun tubs. (US Army)

An LVT(A)-4 of the Marine 3rd Armored Amphibian Battalion on the beach at Peleliu on 15 September 1944. Due to the amtanks' very light armour, the Marines preferred to land M4A2 medium tanks as soon as possible to provide direct fire support for the advance inland from the beach. (USMC)

the amtanks were, and tended to use them in the same way that they would use an M4A2 Sherman tank. The controversy over the issue of whether amtanks should be used to support Marine or Army advances beyond the immediate beach area lingered long after the Marshalls fighting.

The fighting in the Marshalls was not a repeat of the bloody Tarawa experience. The Japanese defenders were much more scattered than on Tarawa, and the Marines and Army had drawn appropriate lessons from the earlier débâcle. The Marines were supported by tanks from the 4th Marine Tank Battalion, and the Army units at Kwajalein were supported by the 767th Tank Battalion. The use of the amtanks in a fire support rôle had revealed some shortcomings, however. The 37mm M6 gun was perfectly adequate to deal with the rarely-encountered Japanese tanks, but it was not suitable for attacking the bunkers or other fortified positions which were a more common target, and so there was a desire for a larger weapon. Two days after the Kwajalein landing, the 4th Marine Division attacked the two adjacent islands of Roi and Namur, using the 4th and 10th Amphibian Tractor Battalions, supported by the 1st Armored Amphibian Battalion.

The LVT(A)-4 Amtank

Development of a more heavily armed amtank, the LVT(A)-4, was in fact already nearing completion. Just as the LVT(A)-1 had been armed with the turret from the M5A1 light tank, so the new LVT(A)-4 was armed with the turret from the M8 75mm Howitzer Motor Carriage (based on the M5A1 light tank chassis). As in the case of the M5A1/M8 HMC, the LVT(A)-4 required a larger turret ring, which meant extending the superstructure back on the LVT(A)-4, covering over the two scarf rings

of the machine-gun tubs: at the time it was not evident to the designers that the deletion of these machine-gun positions would be one of the most serious tactical shortcomings of the new LVT(A)-4.

As well as work on up-gunned versions of the amtanks, work had also begun on other forms of fire support amtracs and amtanks. Prototypes of LVT(A)-1s with E7 and E14-7R2 flame-throwers were developed, but were never accepted for deployment to the Pacific. Ironically, the lack of flamethrower amtracs had led the Army's 708th Amphibian Tank Battalion to build five improvised flame amtracs by mounting ordinary infantry man-pack M1 flamethrowers in a small opening in the bow of some LVT(A)-2s and LVT(A)-1s. These were used during the Kwajalein operation, but were not very useful since their range was inadequate. The Army's 2nd Engineer Special Brigade Support Battery modified a number of LVT(A)-2s into fire support vehicles. Each amtrac received four Mk VII 4.5in. barrage rocket projectors, three M2 .50-cal. heavy machine-guns, and a pedestal-mounted Mk IV 37mm automatic cannon (like that used on the P-39 fighter). The Marines developed similar rocket-firing amtracs in the Central Pacific fighting, but generally landing craft were used in this rôle rather than amtracs.

With the exception of a small number of Army LVT(A)-2s, all amtracs were built unarmoured despite the implications drawn from Tarawa. The Navy was reluctant to armour all amtracs, since many, would continue to be used in a logistical support rôle where more armour meant that less cargo could be carried. Instead, standardised armour kits were developed to be welded to amtracs used in assault landings. The kits contained cut sheets of half and quarter-inch steel. The half-inch steel was welded to the bow and front cab, while the quarter-inch panels were added to the pontoons. Some units in the field added additional plates of their own. Beginning in March 1944, all LVT-2s had cab armour added at the factory. The armour used on LVTs during the war was only sufficient to protect against small arms fire. Shrapnel and heavy machine-gun fire could penetrate the pontoons, and crews had to carefully check the side pontoons before entering the water again to prevent the vehicle from filling with water and sinking. (Crews were issued a bag of wooden plugs to hammer into any holes they found.)

Battle for the Marianas

The main campaign in the Central Pacific, for the key Marianas islands of Saipan, Guam and Tinian, was scheduled for June–July, 1944. These operations were to be the largest amphibious landings using amtracs to date. The first LVT(A)-4 amtanks and LVT-4 amtracs were available for these operations. The Army's 708th Amphibian Tank Battalion had 16 LVT(A)-4s, issuing each tank company four LVT(A)-4s and 13 LVT(A)-1s; while the Marines' new 2nd Armored Amphibian Battalion was almost entirely equipped with the newer amtank. Operation 'Forager', the attack on Saipan, began on 15 June 1944. About 700 amtracs were used, including amtanks from the Army's 708th Amphibian Tank Battalion and the Marines' 2nd Armored Amphibian Battalion, and six amtrac battalions including the Army's 534th, 715th and 773rd and the Marines' 2nd, 4th and 10th Amphibian Tractor Battalions.

By the time of the Saipan operation, Japanese tactics were changing: they had decided to avoid placing most of their defensive positions on the beaches, realising that many would be lost to the heavy US naval bombardment. Instead, on larger islands, defences were planned to take advantage of terrain features inland. The landings at Saipan were not contested in the same fashion as at Tarawa, but the Japanese forces launched a number of counter-attacks against the beach-head, including tank attacks. The 708th Amphibian Tank Battalion particularly distinguished itself during the fighting, earning the Presidential Unit

A wave of Marine LVT(A)-4s advance towards the beaches at Iwo Jima. The least popular feature of the LVT(A)-4 was its vulnerability to close-in infantry attack due to its lack of roof armour, and insufficient machine-guns. By the time of the Iwo Jima landing this had been ameliorated by adding more machine-guns and gun shields, as seen here. (USMC)

Citation. Saipan was declared secure on 9 July 1944; and on 27 July Guam and Tinian were attacked. As at Saipan, the initial landings were conducted using amtracs. The attack on Guam on 21 July 1944 involved 358 amtracs and amtanks from the Marines' 1st and 2nd Armored Amphibian Battalions and the 3rd and 4th Amphibian Tractor Battalions. The attack on Tinian included an initial assault by 465 Army and Marine amtracs and 68 amtanks. Tinian's beaches proved more of a problem due to the presence of coral cliffs at the edge of the beach area, so a special Seebee version of the LVT-2, the Doodlebug, was fitted with a timber ramp over the top of the vehicle to permit following amtracs to surmount the barrier. Ten Doodlebugs were built by the Marine 2nd Amphibian Tractor Battalion, proving to be quite successful during their brief employment at Tinian.

The Marianas campaign reflected a gradual maturing of assault amphibian doctrine. Many of the amtrac battalion officers presented detailed suggestions for improvements on the vehicles in their after-action reports. The single most common criticism concerned the lack of armour on the amtracs, and the lack of armour kits to protect machine-gun positions on the vehicles. As an interim solution armour shields were improvised, or Navy small craft or landing craft shields were obtained. There was also some dissatisfaction with the general configuration of the existing LVT-2 amtrac: to disembark, the troops had to leap over the sides – a dangerous procedure in a contested beach-head. Solutions to some of these problems were already underway back in the United States.

The Marianas fighting highlighted problems with the amtanks. The LVT(A)-1 was generally viewed as being unsuitable; the 37mm gun was

Army troops of the 7th Infantry Division in an LVT-4 move towards the beach at Okinawa on D-Day, 1 April 1945. The LVT-4 had a large rear ramp, as seen here, which permitted easier loading and unloading of the cargo bay than the earlier LVT-1 and LVT-2 amtracs. (US Army)

The rolling countryside of Okinawa permitted large-scale mechanised operations. Amtracs and amtanks, like these Marine LVT(A)-4s, were used to transport and support these Marine drives. (USMC)

not very useful against bunkers, and Japanese tanks were so rarely encountered on the beach that its anti-armour ability was seldom needed. The one good feature of the LVT(A)-1 was the provision of the two scarf ring mounts for .30-cal. machine-guns on the rear hull. The Japanese infantry lacked any advanced anti-armour weapons like bazookas, and so were obliged to attack tanks using suicidal tactics with magnetic mines. Close-in defence of the amtanks against such attacks was vital.

The LVT(A)-4 was welcomed for its larger gun; the short 75mm howitzer was a much more useful weapon than the 37mm anti-tank gun on the LVT(A)-1. However, the LVT(A)-4 had been developed with little appreciation of the type of fighting taking place in the Pacific; it lacked the two rear machine-gun tubs of the LVT(A)-1, and had no co-axial .30-cal. machine-gun fitted beside the 75mm howitzer. Its only self-defence weapon was a .50-cal. M2 HB heavy machine-gun fitted to a ring mount on top of the turret. From this position, the machine-gunner was completely exposed to enemy small arms fire. The LVT(A)-4 was thus much more difficult to defend than the LVT(A)-1; and in fact many amtank crews felt that machine-guns were actually the most valuable element of the amtanks in many circumstances. Another unpopular feature on the LVT(A)-4 was the lack of overhead armour on the turret – a particular shortcoming in areas of heavy foliage where concealed Japanese troops and snipers could fire or throw grenades into the turret.

Apart from listing the equipment shortcomings, the officers of the 708th Amphibian Tank Battalion suggested that the rôle of amtanks be changed to that of mobile artillery, and that further training should be provided for amtank crews to prepare them for the use of their vehicles in an indirect fire rôle. They also noted that once the beach was secured

The LVT-3C Bushmaster had the rear cargo bay covered over, and a turret added in the front. This rear view shows the detail changes on the LVT-3C. (Author's collection)

and tanks landed, tanks would be better suited to direct-fire actions and close infantry support than the thinly armoured amtanks. The after-action reports from the amtank units recommended that the LVT(A)-1 be withdrawn from service, and that an improved version of the LVT(A)-4 take its place.

The criticisms of the LVT(A)-4 were taken to heart, although not all the recommendations were approved for production vehicles. An improved version of the LVT(A)-4 was developed, and although it was not given an official designation, it was popularly called the LVT(A)-4 'Marianas Model', after the campaign which had prompted its development. The rear of the turret was modified by removing the small partial roof and the ring mount along with the .50-cal. heavy machine-gun: in its place, two pintle-mounted .30-cal. machine-guns were added, complete with gun shields. A ballmounted .30-cal. machine-gun was added in the superstructure front (although this feature had been developed before the Marianas campaign, and had been added on late-production LVT(A)-1s as well). Few of the LVT(A)-4 Marianas Models were available in the Pacific until 1945; and as a result there was a good deal of improvisation on LVT(A)-4s to provide protection for the turret machine-gunner, and to add additional machine-guns. Further improvements, including a power traverse system for the turret and a gyro-stabiliser for the howitzer, led in 1945 to the LVT(A)-5. Development of an amtank with even better armament, the T86 Amphibian Gun Carriage, was begun by the Army in 1943. This was basically an attempt to develop an amphibian version of the M18 tank destroyer. A corresponding howitzer version with a 105mm howitzer, the T87, also reached prototype form. However, by the time that these vehicles were ready for production in late 1944, there was little Army, or Marine Corps interest in amtanks.

New amtracs

The LVT Continuing Board had already recognised the shortcomings in amtrac configuration in 1942. The need to use a crane to load and unload cargo from the centre hold of the LVT-2 limited its utility, but due to wartime priorities LVT-2 production continued, while the LVT

Continuing Board and the Navy proceeded with improved variants.

In the spring of 1942, the LVT Continuing Board was sponsoring two development programmes to improve the automotive performance of the LVT-1. The project by FMC, which led to the LVT-2 design, envisioned keeping the central cargo hold configuration, but greatly improving the track and suspension. The LVT-2 was ready for production at the end of 1942, and went into series production in January 1943. With the LVT-2 design completed in the spring of 1942, FMC turned to the development of a further derivative with a reconfigured cargo hold, which would eventually become the LVT-4. This new vehicle had the engine moved forward to permit the cargo hold to be located aft, accessible by a large ramp door. This configuration permitted the LVT-4 to load and unload cargo rapidly, and it could easily carry wheeled equipment such as jeeps or small artillery pieces. The first large order for the LVT-4 was placed in November 1943; the first series production LVT-4s were completed in December 1943, and they first entered service at the time of the Saipan landing in June 1944. The LVT-4 was produced in larger numbers than any other type of amtrac during the war, representing almost half of all amtrac production. However, it arrived on the scene relatively late, and so only saw widespread use in 1945. The Marines and Army discussed manufacturing a version constructed of armour steel, comparable to the LVT(A)-2 amtrac. This was designated the LVT(A)-3, but it was never approved for production, and optional armour kits were issued in its place to armour the regular LVT-4.

The second programme being sponsored by the LVT Continuing Board was to emerge as the LVT-3. In 1942 the Navy's Bureau of Ships approached the Morse Chain Company, a division of Borg-Warner Corporation, to develop a new track and suspension system to replace the primitive type used on the LVT-1 Alligator. Borg-Warner suggested that a more prudent course would be to redesign the vehicle entirely, to

The LVTP-X3, designed by FMC in 1947, was one of a number of experimental amtracs developed immediately after the war in an attempt to examine new approaches and configurations. None of these entered production until the Korean War forced the Navy to replace the LVT-3C. (FMC Corp.)

which the Navy agreed. This resulted in the Borg-Warner Amphibian, Model A, which was delivered to the LVT Continuing Board in Florida in August 1942 for trials. The Borg-Warner Amphibian, Model A was developed as a convertible amtrac/amtank. A weapons module, mounting the turret from an M3A1 Stuart light tank, could be bolted or unbolted to the chassis to convert it to and from a cargo carrier or an amphibious tank. The Model A proved successful in tests, but it was not approved for production since it offered no significant improvement over the existing LVT-2 Water Buffalo, or its amtank derivative, the LVT(A)-1.

Nevertheless, the Model A had displayed a number of innovations in track and suspension, and the Navy authorised Borg-Warner to proceed with an improved type, the Model B. The Model B programme started at the same time that the LVT Continuing Board had been sponsoring the LVT-4, with its emphasis on easier access to the cargo hold. Likewise, the Model B was designed with a rear ramp for access to the rear-mounted cargo hold. One of the main innovations in the Model B design was the shifting of the two 110hp Cadillac engines (from the M5/M5A1 tank) into the hull sponsons, leaving more space in the internal cargo hold. Trials of the Model B took place at Camp Pendleton, California, a year later in August 1943. The initial prototype was constructed with armour plate, but after trials the Navy requested that it be manufactured with sheet steel, with an optional armour kit. The modified Model B was accepted for production in March 1944, and

Development of a smaller amtrac, the FMC LVTP-6, paralleled development of the Borg-Warner LVTP-5. Based on the Army M59 APC, the LVTP-6 never entered quantity production. (FMC Corp.)

an initial order was placed for 1,800 vehicles. It was type-classified as the LVT-3. The Marines felt that production of a wholly new type was justified due to the suspension and powertrain improvements offered by the LVT-3 Bushmaster over the older LVT-2/LVT-4 Water Buffalo Family. The LVT-3 did not see combat until 1945 at Okinawa.

LATE-WAR LANDINGS

The Palaus

The next target in the island-hopping campaign in the Central Pacific was the Palau group in the Caroline Islands. The main Japanese base at Peleliu was assigned to the Marines, while the Army helped tackle neighbouring Anguar Island. Peleliu threatened to be another Tarawa, with heavy Japanese defences and fortifications. By the time of Peleliu, Japanese defensive tactics had continued their shift away from the reliance on heavy beach defences and wasteful *banzai* charges against the beach-head. Instead, the Peleliu garrison – four times the size of the Tarawa garrison – burrowed into the rocky ridges further inland.

By this time Marine tactics, too, had greatly improved. The main problem was that there were not enough amtracs to go around. The 1st Marine Division hoped to have one amtrac battalion per regiment against the three beaches, plus an amtank battalion to lead the wave. It had the 1st and 8th Amphibian Tractor Battalions, and the 3rd Armored Amphibian Battalion with LVT(A)-1s and LVT(A)-4s. At the last moment, a shipment of about 50 of the new LVT-4s arrived; these were used to form a provisional battalion, causing a certain amount of disruption, since one of the battalions was relatively new and inexperienced, and many of the crews in the provisional unit were completely untrained.

On 15 September 1944 the three amtrac battalions were preceded to the beach by the amtank battalion and by rocket-launching landing craft to soften up Japanese positions. The initial approach was far less costly than at Tarawa; but once the surrounding reef was reached casualties mounted, eventually totalling 26 amphibians. The terrain of the beach area was badly torn up by the naval bombardment, and was thus unsuitable for the use of amtanks. As a result of the earlier cautious use of amtanks on Saipan, the 1st Marine Division insisted this time on having tanks land as soon as possible, rather than depend entirely on the amtanks for initial fire support. About 30 Shermans of the 1st Tank Battalion were landed, and proved instrumental in securing the beach.

Prior to the landings, three of the new LVT-4s had been modified as flamethrower vehicles, mounting Navy Mk. 1 (Ronson) flame guns. They stood unused for the first two days of fighting; but on the third day they began to be brought forward to rout out Japanese fortifications, and they were used later in the campaign when a small amtrac and amtank task force was sent off to neighbouring Ngesbus island to attack the Japanese garrison there. The landings at Anguar Island on 17 September were conducted by the Army's 726th Amphibian Tractor Battalion, supported by the 776th Amphibian Tank Battalion.

Marine casualties on Peleliu were double those on Tarawa, and it proved to be a very controversial operation. However, defenders in four times the strength of the Betio garrison had been overcome, and the landings had been conducted without serious blunders. In many respects, Peleliu marked the culmination in the development of marine amphibian assault operations in World War II. By this stage, the central rôle of the amtracs in the initial landing had been well established by the successes at Guam, Saipan and Peleliu, and the rôle of amtanks in providing initial fire support was also accepted. The importance of amtanks in amphibious landings was viewed with some ambivalence, however, both in the amtank battalions, and in the Marine divisions themselves. With the improvement in tank wading equipment, conventional tanks could be landed on the beaches within half an hour of the initial landings. No one, especially the amtank crews, questioned the fact that the M4A2 Shermans were much better suited to providing close-in direct fire support for the Marines once ashore. The importance of amtanks in amphibious operations therefore continued to decline as the rôle of conventional tanks increased. Once ashore, they were used mainly in the indirect artillery fire support rôle while conventional tanks were used for direct fire support.

The Philippines

The largest single use of amtracs and amtanks in the Pacific war, the Leyte landings on 20 October 1944, are perhaps the least famous. The US Army used nine amtrac and two amtank battalions for the landing, but there was no contest for the beaches. As a result, the Army amtracs were reduced to their initial rôle of logistical support, and little attention was paid to the landings. The Army retained a large number of amtracs for use in landings on the many islands in the Philippines, using two amtrac battalions in the landing at Ormoc Island on 7 December 1944 and four at Lingayen Gulf on Luzon on 9 January 1945.

Iwo Jima

If there were questions about the need to take Peleliu, there were no such doubts about Iwo Jima. This small volcanic island was viewed as essential to help support bomber operations against Japan, and the eventual mainland landings planned for 1946. A total of 482 LVTs made the initial landings, including the 4th and 5th Amphibian Tractor Battalions, and the LVT(A)-4s of the 2nd Armored Amphibian Battalion. As at Peleliu, the Japanese had shifted to a more cautionary defence, preferring to wage costly defensive actions from fortifications and bunkers away from the beach rather than face a hailstorm of fire on the beach itself. As a result, the amtracs were able to make the beach without suffering serious losses. Once they were on the beach, however, the Japanese artillery and mortars took their toll of vehicles and men; so tank support was landed almost immediately, and played a central rôle in routing out Japanese bunkers. Iwo Jima was undoubtedly the toughest Marine battle of the war, fought against a garrison ten times the size of Tarawa and even better fortified, but the assault landings did not match Tarawa in bloody ferocity. The rôle of amtanks continued to diminish: with an adequate supply of tanks on Iwo Jima they were relegated to an artillery support rôle, for which they were better suited.

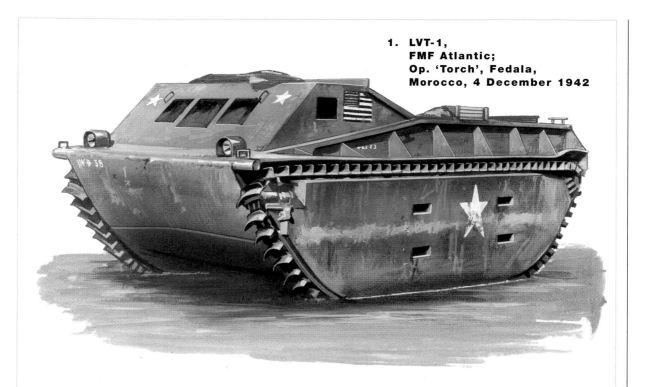

1. **LVT-1,**
   FMF Atlantic;
   Op. 'Torch', Fedala,
   Morocco, 4 December 1942

2. **LVT-1,**
   US Marine
   2nd Amphibian Tractor Battalion;
   Tarawa, 20 November 1943

1. **LVT-4,**
   11th Royal Tank Regiment;
   Elbe River, Germany, 29 April 1945

2. **LVT(A)-1,**
   708th Amphibian Tank Battalion,
   US Army; Saipan, 15 June 1944

1. LVT-2,
US Marine
4th Amphibian Tractor
Battalion;
Iwo Jima, 1945

2. LVT-3,
US Marine
1st Amphibious Tractor Battalion;
Hungnam Harbour, Korea,
December 1950

LANDING VEHICLE TRACKED (ARMOURED) LVT(A)-4

KEY

1 Water propulsion flow gates
2 Engine intake water covers
3 Fuel filler cap
4 Vehicle engine
5 Turret tarpaulin stowage
6 Turret race
7 .50-cal. machine ammunition drum
8 .50-cal. M2 heavy machine-gun
9 Machine-gun scarf ring
10 Howitzer protective cage
11 Turret
12 75mm M3 howitzer in M7 mount
13 Howitzer panoramic sight
14 Gun mantlet
15 Gun mantlet barrel cover
16 Driver's seat
17 Driver's hatch
18 Driver's periscope attachment
19 Driver's controls
20 Vehicle light
21 Boat hook
22 Powertrain transmission
23 .30-cal. hull machine-gun
24 Drive sprocket
25 Radio antenna
26 Co-driver/hull machine-gunner seat
27 Vehicle radio
28 Powertrain tunnel
29 Return roller
30 Alternate radio antenna pot
31 Track with integral grouser
32 Lifting hook
33 Torsilastic bogie wheel
34 Buoyancy pontoon
35 Idler wheel
36 Fender
37 Rear protective bumper
38 Air vent louvres into fighting compartment
39 Tow cable

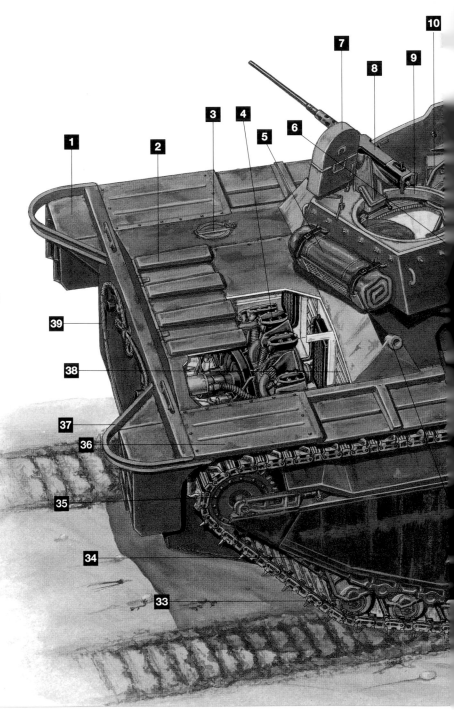

SPECIFICATIONS

Crew: 4
Combat weight: 35,100lbs empty
Power-to-weight ratio: 12.5hp/t
Overall length: 26.1ft
Width: 10.2ft
Engine: 250hp Continental W-670-9A
  7 cylinder radial

Transmission: Synchromesh (5F, 1R),
  controlled differential steering,
  herringbone gear final drive
Fuel capacity: 106 gallons
Maximum speed (road): 25mph
Maximum speed (water): 7mph
Maximum range: 125 miles (road),
  75 miles (water)

Fuel consumption: 0.85 gallons per mile (road)
Fording depth: Amphibious
Armour: 51mm (turret front); 25mm (turret sides);
  6mm (hull sides, rear)
Armament: 75mm howitzer M3
Main gun ammunition: M4 high-explosive with Charge 4
Muzzle velocity: 1,250ft/s
Maximum effective range: 9,620 yards
Stowed main gun rounds: 100 rounds
Gun depression/elevation: –20 to +40°

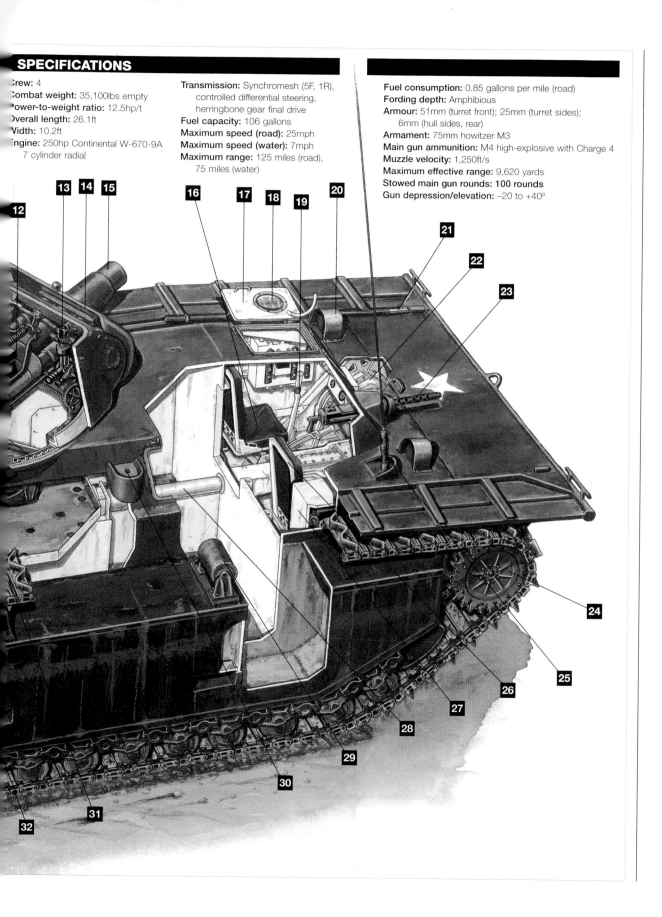

1. LVTE-1,
3rd Amphibious Tractor Battalion,
1st US Marine Division;
Vietnam, 1967

2. LVTH-6,
Taiwanese Marine Division;
Taiwan, 1983

**1. LVTP-7,
Transport Company,
Battaglione Marina 'San Marco';
Italy, 1984**

**2. LVTP-7,
Argentine 1st Amphibious Vehicle Battalion;
Falklands, April 1982**

1. LVTP-7,
   US Marine 2nd Amphibious Assault Company;
   Grenada, 26 October 1983

2. LVTP-7,
   US Marine 6th Amphibious Brigade;
   Italy, 1985

The LVTE-1 'Potato Digger' was used for engineer support and mine-field breaching. It is fitted with a combination bulldozer blade/mine rake in the front. The large structure on the roof is the launcher for the rocket-propelled demolition line charge. (FMC Corp.)

Okinawa

Okinawa proved to be the climactic battle of the Pacific War, placing US forces on the doorstep of the Japanese Home Islands. The initial landings on 1 April 1945 were preceded by a number of amphibious assaults against smaller islands in the Ryukyus by US Army troops who seized anchorages for the US Navy, and cleared out Japanese garrisons on the Okinawa approaches. The Okinawa landings – which were not contested – were carried out by four divisions, two Army and two Marine, supported by nearly a dozen amtrac and amtank battalions. Amtracs played an unanticipated rôle in the fighting, being used by the Marines for prolonged mechanised infantry operations, akin to the Army's use in Europe of armoured infantry half-tracks. Okinawa's rolling hills permitted the use of amtracs to carry troops deep inland.

Okinawa was not the last use of amtracs in the Pacific, though it was certainly the last major operation. They were used in the Mindanao landings in the Philippines on 17 April 1945; at Lake Santerne on New Guinea on 24 April 1945; at the Bongac Channel on Sulu on 27 April; at Cebu in the Philippines on 26 May 1945; and finally, in a large operation involving two US Army amtrac battalions at Balikpapan in Borneo on 1 July 1945. This last operation also marked one of the only uses of amtracs by other Allied troops during the Pacific fighting. The Australians had formed the 1st Amphibious Armoured Squadron using newly arrived LVT(A)-4s, and the 1st Australian Tracked Amphibious Vehicle Platoon AASC in February 1945. The US supplied a total of 30 LVT(A)-4s and about 300 LVT-4s to Australia and China in 1945. Although neither unit was to see action, Australian troops involved in the Balikpapan landings did use LVTs in small numbers; as did British forces in Burma.

AMTRACS IN EUROPE

Although amtracs are much more closely associated with the fighting in the Pacific, they were used in a number of operations in the European theatre as well. However, priority was always given to the Pacific units, and LVTs did not become available in Europe in significant numbers until the late summer of 1944. The US supplied 200 LVT-1s to Britain in 1943, which were used mainly for training and experimentation. These were followed by 100 LVT-2s and 203 LVT-4s in 1944, and 50 LVT(A)-4s in 1945 under the Lend–Lease programme. These were called Buffalo II (LVT-2) and Buffalo IV (LVT-4) in British service (or Fantails, in Italy). Not surprisingly, the unit most closely associated with amtrac employment in the European theatre was the British 79th Armoured Division, which was already renowned for its work with specialised armoured vehicles. In October 1944 the 79th Armoured Division was assigned the messy task of dislodging German forces in the Scheldt estuary who were blocking the approaches to the vital port of Antwerp. LVTs of the 1st Assault Brigade, Royal Engineers were used to land troops on South Beveland Island on 23/24 October followed by an attack on Walcheren. Walcheren was protected by dikes, which the Allies ruptured to complicate the defence of the Germans. The 11th RTR and the 5th Assault Regiment RE were fitted out with LVT-2 and LVT-4 Buffaloes for the operation, to carry troops and equipment in the assault. After the 1 November 1944 landing, it took a week of bloody fighting to secure the island. The 11th RTR was again employed with Buffaloes at the Rhine crossing on 7 March 1945. Besides using the LVT-4s in the conventional rôle, the division developed some specialised derivatives, including a mat-laying LVT-4 which could place a carpet of wire-linked logs on the muddy shore-banks to help DD tanks and other amphibious vehicles transit the river approaches without becoming bogged down; and the Sea Serpent, an LVT-4 fitted with two small turrets and flame guns. In view of the possibility of the British Army becoming more involved in amphibious operations in the Pacific at the conclusion of the European war, a requirement for a British amtrac became apparent, and development began in the spring of 1944. Designed by Morris Commercial Cars, it was heavily based on the LVT-4, but was somewhat larger. It was dubbed the 'Amphibian, tracked, 4 ton GS', better known as Neptune. A total of 2,000 were ordered, along with a recovery version (Sealion) and workshop version (Turtle); but with the end of the war the contracts were cancelled after only a handful had been completed.

The US Army used LVT-2s and LVT-4s in small numbers in 1944 and 1945 for river crossing operations. One of the largest joint US–UK operations using amtracs in Europe took place along the Po River in Italy in March–April 1945 under the control of the British 9th Armoured Brigade. The US 755th Tank Battalion was converted to a Fantail unit with 119 LVTs for the operation. Likewise, an RASC unit and the 2/7th Lancers were outfitted with LVTs from US sources. The LVTs were used to cross flooded areas south of Lake Comacchio as part of Operation 'Impact' on 11 April 1945, followed by Operation 'Impact Royal' two days later; and on 24–26 April, Company C of the 755th Tank Battalion was used in landing operations across the Po River.

The LVTE-7 was accepted for service, but did not enter production. The device on the rear of the vehicle is the rocket launcher assembly which was used to launch demolition line charges for minefield breaching. (FMC Corp.)

POST-WAR LVT DEVELOPMENT

By the end of the war the Navy had ordered 22,683 amtracs and amtanks of the standard production models. However, in late 1945 the Navy cancelled many of these contracts, and a total of 18,621 LVTs were delivered. The accompanying charts provide more comprehensive details of the wartime production of LVTs.

Following the war, the Army gradually withdrew from amphibious assault vehicle development, and disbanded its amphibian tank and tractor battalions. Many of the amtanks and amtracs that had been supplied to the Army were turned over to allies, notably to China and France. Many Marine and Army amtracs located overseas were simply broken up for scrap.

The US Marine Corps, realising that budget limits made the acquisition of new amtracs unlikely, decided to hold on to the newest production vehicles, notably the LVT-3 amtracs and LVT(A)-5 amtanks, most of which had not been shipped from the US before the war ended. In 1949 plans were begun to modernise the LVT-3 by adding overhead armour to protect the troop bay; and this was carried out in 1950 on 1,200 LVT-3s by Continental Aviation & Engineering (CA&E), resulting in the LVT-3C. These formed the backbone of Marine amtrac units in Korea. There were plans to develop a heavily modernised LVT(A)-5, and two very different prototypes were completed by CA&E and FMC in 1949. In 1951 a small number of LVT(A)-5s were modified by FMC with a new bow, turret roof armour, and other changes; and some of these saw service in Korea.

Apart from the modernisation programme on existing LVTs in the inventory, the US Navy Bureau of Ships was also engaged in an active

The LVT-7A1 new production vehicles are easily distinguished from the LVT-7 series and the LVT-7A1 SLEP vehicles by the square housings for the front headlights and the raised commander's cupola. This is an LVTC-7A1, evident from the extra radio antennae and the lack of a machine-gun turret. (FMC Corp.)

programme of LVT technology development. In the late 1940s a series of LVT prototypes were built by various manufacturers under Navy contract to examine new hull, suspension and propulsion concepts. Many prototype vehicles, including new amtanks, amtracs and specialised cargo vehicles, were built and tested, none of them progressing beyond the prototype stage, the intention being merely to examine new LVT technologies. Funding for actual production was simply not available.

LVTs return to combat

LVTs were back in combat shortly after the end of the Second World War. The Communist and Nationalist Chinese waged a brutal civil war, finally culminating in the expulsion of the Nationalist Chinese forces from the mainland onto the island of Taiwan. The Nationalist Chinese forces were provided with a number of LVTs, mainly the LVT(A)-4 and LVT-4, from US Army and Marine stockpiles, which were used extensively in combat, many later being captured (and used) by Communist Chinese forces.

The outbreak of war in Korea caught the US Marine Corps and Army unprepared. Not surprisingly, the US Marine forces in Korea requested that their amtrac battalions be brought back up to strength, and the 1st Amphibian Tractor Battalion was equipped with the newly modernised LVT-3C. On 15 September this unit, supported by LVT(A)-5s of the 56th Amphibian Tank and Tractor Battalion, were used in the landing at Inchon – which dramatically affected the course of the war. LVT-3Cs also figured prominently in Marine attacks over the Han River later in the month, and in the evacuation of Hungnam Harbour following the Chinese entry into the war.

1950 also marked the entry of the LVTs into another Asian war. French forces in Indochina had been using US M29C Weasels, known as *crabes* to the French, in the watery terrain of the deltas. Perhaps the best known of these formations was the battalion raised by the 1er Régiment Étrangère de Cavalerie in 1948. Until 1950, the US had been unwilling to support the French effort in Indochina militarily, viewing it as an undesirable remnant of archaic colonialism. Once the States became enmeshed in the war in Korea, however, the Indochina fighting was suddenly viewed in a new light; as another element in the containment of Communism. The US began supplying the French with equipment that had previously been denied, including LVT-4 and LVT(A)-4 amphibians. The first of these arrived in November 1950, and were used by the Foreign Legion cavalry to form the 1er Sous-groupement Amphibie, the first of a number of amphibious assault groups. The LVTs proved to be ideally suited to the delta, providing waterborne transport in deep water, and acceptable mobility on the murky soil of rice-paddies and riverbanks. In 1951, when more vehicles became available, the 1er REC formed two amphibious groups, comprised of two Crab squadrons with 33 machine-gun armed Crabs each, three Alligator squadrons for troop transport with 11 LVT-4s each, and a support platoon, with six LVT(A)-4s. The Foreign Legion cavalry were particularly successful in their use of these unique units, employing them imaginatively in spite of the poor terrain. To provide even more firepower, some LVT-4s were modified to carry 40mm Bofors anti-aircraft guns for infantry support. Most of the French LVT-4s were armed with shielded machine-guns, or recoilless rifles and mortars.

The end of the Indochina War did not signal the end of French amtrac operations. During the 1956 planning for the seizure of the Suez Canal, the Anglo–French planning committee decided to use amtracs to effect a landing at Port Faud. As Britain no longer had any Lend–Lease amtracs available, the French Navy improvised an amphibious assault group from the former Amphibious Center at Arzew, then in the process of being re-formed as the Marine Brigade. They were used to land the 1er REP and 3eme Marine Commando opposite the police and coast-guard stations at Port Faud during the landings. Both LVT-4 amtracs and LVT(A)-4 amtanks were employed.

The LVTP-5

With the conclusion of the war in Korea, Marine amphibian tractor units were in poor condition with a total of 539 LVTs of various models returning from Korea in a particularly bad way. They were rebuilt yet again at the Mare Island Navy Yard, but were fast approaching the end of their useful life. The LVTs that were in better shape were delivered to allied marine forces under the MAP programme, notably to the Taiwanese and South Korean marines. It was clear that a new LVT would be required.

At the outbreak of the Korean War, the Navy Bureau of Ships had decided to press ahead with a new LVT programme based on the technology development efforts it had been conducting since 1946. In December 1950 it issued a contract to the Ingersoll Products Division of

Borg–Warner Corporation to develop a new family of amtracs. The aim was to design a basic troop carrier (LVTP-5), an artillery fire support vehicle (LVTH-6), a command and radio vehicle (LVTCR-1), an air defence vehicle (LVTAA-1), a recovery vehicle (LVTR-1) and a combat engineer/minefield breaching vehicle (LVTE-1). What was remarkable about the new amtrac was its size: it weighed 35 tons unloaded, and was designed to carry 30–34 combat-armed troops – nearly double the complement of previous amtracs.

The first prototype, of an LVTH-6 gun carrier, was completed in August 1951. Interestingly enough, in 1951 FMC suggested the development of a smaller amtrac family, called the Medium-weight LVTP-X2. The FMC entry was essentially a navalised version of the armoured troop carrier it was designing for the Army, and which would eventually emerge as the M59 APC. The Army was insisting that all of its new troop carriers be amphibious, and the M59 was capable of swimming across small rivers or lakes. However, the Army requirement for amphibious capability was far less demanding than the Navy requirement. The Navy standards for amtracs insisted that they be able to negotiate heavy surf and to survive submergence in heavy sea conditions; they also expected far higher water speeds, and better manoeuvrability in water. As a result, the M59 had to be substantially rebuilt to improve its buoyancy and its water propulsion characteristics.

Trials of the Borg–Warner amtracs were successful, and in 1952 production began on the LVTP-5 troop carrier and the LVTH-6 gun carrier. In spite of the decision to press ahead with production of the LVTP-5, the Marines decided to continue development of the smaller (and cheaper) FMC LVTP-X2, feeling that such a design might complement the LVTP-5. As in the LVTP-5 family, a gun carrier and air defence version were developed, as well as a troop carrier. In 1956 the FMC design was accepted for Marine service as the LVTP-6, but by this time the production of the LVTP-5 was almost complete and so the LVTP-6 was never placed into production. A total of 1,124 LVTP-5s and 210 LVTH-6s were built during the period up to 1957. Once production was completed, however, it was decided to convert 58 of the LVTP-5s into command vehicles, designated LVTP-5(Cmd). Small numbers of the LVTE-1 engineer vehicle and 65 LVTR-1 recovery vehicles were also built; but no LVTAA-1 air defence vehicles were built apart from the prototype.

A number of suspension and powertrain problems plagued the early LVTP-5 family, and delayed their initial deployment until 1956. The LVTP-5 series used the same transmission as the M47 and M48 tanks, and due to the powertrain configuration the final drives were about 3ft below the transmission output shafts, requiring a dropgear assembly to couple the final drives and transmissions. The dropgears and early final drives were a frequent source of mechanical failures. Improvements to the powertrain and suspension, as well as other modifications including the addition of a box snorkel and top deck ventilators, solved some of these problems, and the modified vehicles were designated LVTP-5A1, LVTH-6A1, etc.

Marine amphibian tractor battalions of this period had a total of 120 LVTs each. The two tractor companies had four platoons each with 11 LVTP-5A1s. The battalion HQ had three LVTP-5A1 (Cmd) command vehicles; one LVTR-1A1 recovery vehicle; a mine clearance platoon with eight LVTE-1 'Potato Diggers'; a maintenance platoon with one LVTR-1A1; and an amphibian platoon with three LVTP-5A1 (Cmd) and 12 LVTP-5A1 troop carriers. In the 1950s and 1960s, these battalions were organic to the Marine divisions.

Vietnam

During the Vietnam War, the 1st and 3rd Amphibian Tractor Battalions were deployed with the Marines' 3rd and 1st Divisions. The nature of the fighting in Vietnam was ill-suited to traditional amtrac operations, and due to the lack of contested beach assaults the LVTP-5A1s were used, as often as not, as lightly armoured troop carriers. However, the amtracs were very large and bulky and were hardly as suitable for this rôle as the smaller Army M113. Even though they were considerably more durable than amtracs of the Second World War, the LVTP-5s were not intended for prolonged operation on land: the torsilastic suspensions suffered from excessive use for which they were not designed. The powertrain, using a tank engine and transmission rather than a powertrain expressly designed for amtracs, was not ideal, and was difficult to service; a worn-out engine or transmission took nearly a day to replace. The single greatest weakness in the LVTP-5 design was the configuration of the fuel cells in the floor. In Vietnam land mines were the primary danger to armoured vehicles, and a mine detonation under an LVTP-5 often set off the petrol tanks, causing a fiery holocaust in the

The LVTR-7A1 is the recovery version of the LVT-7 series. The hydraulic crane has a 3-ton capacity, and the vehicle is also fitted with a recovery winch of 15-ton capacity. (FMC Corp.)

crew compartment. After a few lethal experiences with this danger, Marine units quickly became accustomed to riding on the outside of the amtracs, feeling that exposure to small arms fire was a lesser risk than the danger posed by mines.

As a result of these problems the use of amtracs was restricted, and efforts were made to tailor their use to the terrain – such as patrolling along riverbanks or coastline, or with Special Landing Teams for coastal operations. They were also used in non-combatant rôles, such as ferrying supplies from rear areas, where their spacious holds proved useful. Besides the basic troop carrier, the other variants of the LVTP-5 series also saw employment in Vietnam. The LVTH-6A1 was intended for use as an indirect artillery fire support vehicle, but in Vietnam over half of its missions were in the tank rôle of direct fire support for Marine units.

The LVTH-6A1 gun carrier was fitted with a 105mm howitzer to provide artillery support during amtrac operations. It could carry 151 rounds of ammunition in racks, plus 150 canistered rounds in the cargo hold, during land operations; but for amphibious use a total of no more than 100 rounds was considered safe. (FMC Corp.)

The LVTP-7

The problems with the LVTP-5 in Vietnam, admittedly caused in large measure by its employment in rôles for which it had not been designed, led to consideration of a replacement. Initial design work for an LVTP-5 replacement had begun in 1964, since the original design specifications for the LVTP-5 had required a 15-year life expectancy, and the vehicles had already been in service since 1955–56. Initial design studies were completed by Chrysler and FMC, and in 1965 FMC won the development contract. The new vehicle, initially designated LVTPX-12, reverted back to the earlier Second World War LVT design in terms of size. Use of the LVTP-5A1 in Vietnam made it clear that such a large vehicle was hardly ideal for land operation; and the crew complement was reduced from 30 to 25 troops (and a three-man crew), or a five-ton payload capacity, on the new vehicle. Greater emphasis was also placed on land performance, in some measure owing to the lesson of Vietnam.

FMC selected a conventional torsion bar suspension in lieu of the torsilastic suspension that had been employed on amtracs since the LVT-2 of 1941. The engine was a well-proven Detroit Diesel truck diesel engine, mated to a new transmission. Propulsion in water was provided by a combination of the normal track propulsion coupled with a new hydrojet system. This offered considerably improved manoeuvrability compared to the sluggish behaviour of previous amtracs. The new vehicle was 15 tons lighter than the LVTP-5. Development took 17 months, and the first vehicle was ready in September 1967. A total of 15 prototypes were constructed, and testing continued throughout 1969. The LVTPX-12 met or surpassed all of its requirements except for the turret weapon station: the initial requirement called for a 20mm cannon armament, but problems with this weapon led to a redesign of the turret with a .50-cal. heavy machine-gun in its place. The new vehicles were first funded in the FY70 (Fiscal Year 1970) defence budget. The new series was designated LVT-7, with the standard troop carrier being designated LVTP-7. The 2nd Amphibious Tractor Battalion at Camp Lejeune, North Carolina received two prototypes for familiarisation in 1971, and initial deliveries of production vehicles began in January 1972.

As with the earlier LVTP-5 series, there were plans to develop a family of related support types based on the LVTP-7. These included the LVTC-7 command vehicle, LVTR-7 recovery vehicle, LVTE-7 minefield breaching vehicle, and LVTH-5 gun carrier. The first three reached prototype form, and the LVTP-7 and LVTC-7 entered production in the early 1970s. The howitzer vehicle, LVTHX-5, was never completed. By the 1970s the Marines had concluded that its fire support rôle could be fulfilled better by M60A1 tanks in the direct fire rôle, and M109 self-propelled 155mm howitzers in the artillery fire support rôle. A total of 942 LVTP-7s, 55 LVTR-7s and 84 LVTC-7s were built in the initial orders for the Marine Corps between 1970 and 1974. By the late 1980s, the Assault Amphibian Battalions were a good deal larger than any previous organisation, having an HQ and Service Company and four Assault Amphibian Companies, totalling 187 LVTP-7s, 15 LVTC-7s and five LVTR-7s.

The LVT-7 family proved more durable and effective in service than the LVTP-5 series. They were cheaper to operate, had much better land and water performance, and could be driven comfortably and for prolonged periods on land without the adverse consequences that had afflicted the LVTP-5's torsilastic suspension. In fact, the LVTP-7's suspension formed the basis for the suspension on the new M2 Bradley Infantry Fighting Vehicle which entered service with the Army in the early 1980s. The LVT-7 series was used operationally by US Marine forces during peacekeeping operations in Lebanon, and in the invasion of Grenada in 1983.

Based on previous experience with amtracs, the Marine Corps expected the LVT-7 series to last about ten years until the mid-1980s, and therefore began development of a successor in the mid-1970s. The Marine Corps considered a number of options, including unconventional approaches such as the LVA armoured air cushion assault vehicle, and the more conventional LVT(X) tracked assault vehicle. The LVA programme envisioned an unorthodox suspension that would use an air cushion system for flotation and propulsion on water, and a track system on land. However, the programme was dropped in 1979, before a prototype was

These LVTP-7s were used during the trials of the new Cadillac Gage turret which was retrofitted to the AAV-7A1s from 1987 onwards. The new turret had both a .50-cal. machine-gun and a 40mm Mk 19 automatic grenade launcher. (Cadillac Gage)

constructed, in favour of pursuing the less costly and risky LVT(X). Three companies – General Dynamics, FMC and Bell Aerospace – received contracts to develop the improved LVT(X).

Into the 1990s: the LVT(X) decision

The LVT(X) programme envisioned an amtrac better suited to land combat than the LVT-7. It would be better armoured, and better armed, with an automatic cannon in the 25–35mm range. In many respects the LVT(X) was planned as a Marine equivalent of the Army's new M2 Bradley Infantry Fighting Vehicle (IFV). Like the Bradley, the troops in the LVT(X) could fight from inside the vehicle, or dismount. To permit the troops to fight from within the vehicle led to some interesting design innovations: Bradley-style firing ports complicated the design of a water-tight hull, so some of the designs relied on two remote control machine-gun turrets at the rear of the vehicle to permit the squad to engage enemy positions. The Marine Corps considered two different LVT(X) configurations; a small 13-troop version, the LVTX-13, and a vehicle more similar in size to the LVTP-7, called the LVTX-21.

One of the more unusual derivatives of the LVT-7 series was the MTU (Mobile Test Unit), a US Army test-bed to consider the feasibility of a medium energy laser for air defence. The circular turret contains the laser beam projector and optical tracking equipment, and the large container on the rear contains the generator needed to supply the prodigious energy requirements of the laser. (US DoD)

The LVT(X) promised to be a fairly expensive vehicle to develop and produce, and many Marine tacticians had grave misgivings about the vehicle's value. It is difficult to balance the conflicting engineering demands for good amphibious capability on the one hand, with good land performance on the other. The LVT(X) would never be as good an infantry fighting vehicle as an IFV designed primarily for land operation. Features necessary for amphibious performance, such as the size requirements for buoyancy and the weight constraints for flotation, conflicted with features for land combat such as a smaller size and heavier armour. Some Marines questioned whether an amtrac was needed any longer. It was no longer clear whether the Pacific island fighting of the Second World War was at all relevant to the rôles which the Marine Corps would face in the 1990s. The LVTP-7 was a perfectly adequate vehicle for such contested landings, and there were other means available for seizing a beach that were not available in 1945. Rather than directly assault a heavily defended beach, the Marines of 1985 could skirt the defences by using heliborne assault. If beaches could be seized without a direct assault using such tactics, other types of craft were far better suited for landing troops and supplies than the amtracs. For example, the Marines were acquiring LCAC air cushion landing craft which could rapidly ferry men, tanks and supplies ashore.

The contingency which most concerned Marine planners in the early 1980s was the possibility of a campaign in the Middle East, such as a war in Iran. In this circumstance, amtracs were irrelevant or ill-suited: landing against a contested beach was unlikely, and the LVTP-7 or LVT(X) were not ideally suited to conducting long mechanised operations in a desert environment. The Marine Corps had fallen behind the US Army in mechanising its forces for prolonged land operations, since its traditional mission focused on beach-head assault. The Army had gone through three generations of armoured infantry carriers since 1941, while the Marines had never been equipped with any. The thought of fighting a Middle East campaign as 'leg infantry' concerned Marine planners: a better solution presented itself in the form of mixed mechanisation of the Marine divisions.

As the LVT-7 had proven so durable, it was in a position to be rebuilt in a Service Life Extension Programme (SLEP) to further extend its usefulness into the 1990s. This allowed the Marines to retain a capability to assault a contested beach Tarawa-fashion. The money saved would be used to purchase armoured infantry transporters for prolonged land campaigns. The Marines decided to adopt a wheeled infantry fighting vehicle, the LAV, to fulfil this latter rôle. As a result of this re-orientation in the configuration of the Marine Corps, the LVT(X) programme was shelved in March 1985 before any prototypes had been completed.

The Marine Corps determined that the existing inventory of LVT-7s would be inadequate to last into the 1990s due to attrition and reorganisation. As a result, an improved version of the LVT-7 designated the LVT-7A1 series was developed, incorporating a number of design improvements. The SLEP programme rebuilt the old vehicles to the new LVT-7A1 standards. A total of 853 LVTP-7s, 77 LVTC-7s and 54 LVTR-7s were rebuilt; and 294 LVTP-7A1s, 29 LVTC-7A1s and ten LVTR-7A1s were newly manufactured in the years 1983–85.

Due to the decision to retain the LVT-7A1 amtracs into the 1990s a number of improvement programmes were also initiated. The Marines were never happy with the armament on the LVTP-7, and in 1984 conducted a number of trials of new weapons turrets. In 1986 the Marines selected a Cadillac-Gage turret armed with both a .50-cal. heavy machine-gun and a Mk 19 40mm grenade launcher. The first 100 conversions

The LVA was an advanced amtrac programme aimed at developing an assault amphibian which would use air cushion propulsion at sea, and tracked propulsion on land. This illustration shows the Bell Aerospace concept of the LVA, showing the air cushion configuration in the background and the retracted air cushion/tracked land configuration in the foreground. The programme promised to be costly and technologically risky, and consequently was abandoned in 1979 before prototypes were completed. (Bell Aerospace)

were funded in Fiscal Year 1987. An LVT-7 hull was experimentally reconfigured as an LVTEX-3 fire support vehicle by adding a surplus Army M551 Sheridan tank turret with a new low-recoil 105mm gun too. In spite of the cancellation of the LWE-7 engineer vehicle, there was still a need for a mine-clearing amtrac to support landing operations. This requirement was partially satisfied by the use of the MCSK (Mine Clearance System Kits) which could be fitted to LVTP-7A1s. This system uses a small rocket to propel a line charge onto a minefield where it is exploded to create a breach. A more elaborate and effective system, called CATFAE, to be fitted to special mine-field breaching vehicles, also underwent development, using a fuel-air explosive rocket. There were also plans to retrofit the LVT-7A1 with P-900 appliqué armour in the late 1980s.

The General Dynamics LVT(X) proposal is seen here in model form. It was armed with a 35mm gun, and had two remote control machine-gun turrets at the rear hull corners. (Author)

AAV-7A1 and FAVC

Due to the reconfiguration of the Marine Corps with its new LAV and LVT units, the USMC decided to change the name of the amtracs to better reflect their intended rôle. Beginning in 1985, the LVT-7AI family was renamed AAV-7A1 (Amphibious Assault Vehicle), ending a 45-year tradition. As durable and long-lived as the AAV-7A1s were hoped to be, it was realised that they would probably have to be replaced some time in the 1990s. As a result, in 1985 the Marine Corps began the FAVC (Future Amphibious Vehicles Concepts) programme. The programme was conducted by the USMC and FMC, and was a two-pronged effort aimed at examining both new amphibious vehicle technologies which could be applied to a modernised AAV-7A1, as well as new vehicle designs.

Foreign amtracs

Both the LVTP-5 and LVT-7 series have been exported in modest numbers, as can be seen on the accompanying chart. The Argentine Marine 1st Amphibious Vehicle Battalion was used in the initial seizure of the Falklands in April 1982, losing one LVTP-7 in the process to anti-tank rockets. The Philippines have used their LVTH-6 and LVTP-5 in amphibious anti-guerrilla operations. The Italian San Marco Marine Battalion was used as part of ITALCON forces during the 1983 Lebanon peacekeeping efforts, along with some of their LVTP-7s.

This is a model of the FMC Future Amphibian Vehicle Concept. The FAVC project was aimed at examining technologies to improve the amphibious qualities of amtracs, including such techniques as retracting streamlined bow panels, side skirts to channel and streamline the tracked suspension, and lengthening the hull with retractable hydrojet tubes. (Joseph Bermudez Jr.)

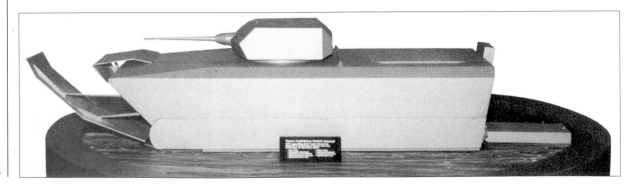

The LVTEX-3 was one of a number of attempts to explore fire support versions of the LVT-7. The Marines had initially planned to acquire the LVTH-5 105mm gun carrier in 1972, but this never progressed beyond the drawing board. The LVTEX-3 mated an experimental Navy 105mm low-recoil gun in a surplus Army M551 Sheridan tank turret. It was not accepted for service use. (US Navy)

LVT production 1941–45

Type	1941	1942	1943	1944	1945	Total
LVT-1	72	851	302			1,225
LVT(A)-1		3	288	219		510
LVT-2			1,540	1,422		2,962
LVT(A)-2			200	250		450
LVT-3			1	733	2,230	2,964
LVT-4			11	4,980	3,360	8,351
LVT(A)-4				1,489	401	1,890
LVT(A)-5					269	269
Totals	72	854	2,342	9,093	6,260	18,621

LVT production by service in World War 2

Type	USMC	US Army	Lend-Lease	Total
LVT-1	540	485	200	1,225
LVT(A)-1	182	328	0	510
LVT-2	1,355	1,507	100	2,962
LVT(A)-2	0	450	0	450
LVT-3	2,962	2	0	2,964
LVT-4	1,765	6,083	503	8,351
LVT(A)-4	533	1,307	50	1,890
LVT(A)-5	128	141	0	269
Totals	7,465	10,303	853	18,621

LVTP-5 and LVTP-7 export

Country	LVT-5 Series	LVTP-7	LVTC-7	LVTR-7
Argentina	0	19	1	1
Brazil	0	16	0	0
Italy	0	24	1	0
Korea	0	53	5	3
Philippines	17	0	0	0
Spain	0	16	2	1
Taiwan	717	0	0	0
Thailand	0	22	0	1
Venezuela	0	9	1	1

THE PLATES

The camouflage painting of US amphibious tractors during the Second World War remains largely unknown. The author has been unable to find painting instructions for amtracs in the records of the US Marine Corps, the US National Archives, or the FMC Corp. archives. From existing colour photos and film, and written accounts, it is evident that the amtracs were originally finished in a blue–grey colour, which the author believes was probably US Navy Ocean Grey. The use of this colour stemmed from the fact that LVTs were initially funded from the US Navy's craft budget. During 1944, there was considerable criticism from Army units that the grey was unsuitable for use once the LVT left the water. As a result, the US Army began to paint its LVTs in Olive Drab around the autumn of 1944. It is not clear whether this was done at the factory or by Army depots. Marine units during this period seem to have resorted to their own measures, adopting locally improvised camouflage. Unfortunately, the battalion records do not mention these activities. Following the war the Marine Corps followed the Army's lead, and painted its amtracs in uniform Forest Green until the mid-1970s, when it adopted the US Army's four-colour MERDC camouflage paint.

An LVT(A)-4 of the Marine 3rd Armored Amphibian Battalion encountered a hidden Japanese gun position on the beach during the landing at Peleliu on 15 September 1944, and knocked it out by ramming it. This is the original version of the LVT(A)-4 with the .50-cal. machine-gun in a ring mount. (USMC)

A1: LVT-1, FMF Atlantic; Operation 'Torch', Fedala, Morocco, 4 December 1942
The vehicle is finished in overall Ocean Grey, and is prominently marked with a large US flag. This marking was carried on most tracked vehicles participating in the landings, and was adopted in the vain hope that the French would not fire on American troops.

A2: LVT-1, US Marine 2nd Amphibian Tractor Battalion; Tarawa, 20 November 1943
This LVT-1 carries a white tactical number marking, as well as the unofficial name 'My De Loris' on the superstructure side.

B1: LVT-4, British 11th Royal Tank Regiment; Elbe River, Germany, 29 April 1945
This LVT-4, manned by 11 RTR, was present on the Elbe

River in the final days of the war. It was finished in overall BSI 987c Olive Drab, a greener colour than the similarly named US Army Olive Drab. The yellow circle insignia is indicative of 'C' Squadron, and the remaining markings are white. Other examples of vehicle names in the troop are 'Southport' and 'Stafford'.

B2: LVT(A)-1, 708th Amphibian Tank Battalion, US Army; Saipan, 15 June 1944

This Army LVT(A)-1 was knocked out during the initial beach fighting at Saipan. It is in overall Ocean Grey. The two yellow stripes on the hull side indicate that it was used at Beach Yellow Two. It is from C Company, as is evident both from the vehicle name ('Crazy Legs') and the bumper code on the front ('C-20'). In the Pacific, many US Army battalions used a battalion insignia in lieu of the bumper code. The battalion insignia of the 708th Amphibian Tank Battalion was a white or yellow triangle with a star in the centre. The 708th Amphibian Tank Battalion also carried a geometric insignia on the turret rear, which may have been a 'wave' marking rather than an individual vehicle marking. In this case, it was a yellow '2' inside a yellow square on the turret rear. It also carries prominent US national insignia, a white star, on the turret side and hull side.

C1: LVT-2, US Marine 4th Amphibian Tractor Battalion; Iwo Jima, 1945

The 4th Marine Division appears to have used a more elaborate and colourful camouflage than in many other units. From colour film of the battle for Iwo Jima it would seem that the 4th Marine Division's armoured vehicles were finished in a pattern of sand, red-brown and dark green. The numbering is in yellow. The initial 'II' is not a number, but rather two yellow stripes, indicating that this amtrac was earmarked for Yellow Beach Two during the attack. The 'B42' is probably a company and vehicle number, although this style of numbering was also occasionally used for 'wave' markings, indicating which initial wave the amtrac would be placed in, and what its position in the wave would be. The number could indicate 4th wave, 2nd vehicle.

C2: LVT-3, US Marine 1st Amphibious Tractor Battalion; Hungnam Harbour, Korea, December 1950

Following the war, Marine amtracs were finished in overall Forest Green, a dark green colour often called 'Marine Green'. The Second World War practice of beach landing markings is still evident on this vehicle, in the form of two red stripes, indicating Red Beach Two. The unit markings are in Chrome Yellow and the national insignia is in white.

D: Landing Vehicle Tracked (Armoured) LVT(A)-4

See cutaway annotations and specification for full details.

E1: LVTE-1, 3rd Amphibious Tractor Battalion, 1st US Marine Division; Vietnam, 1967

Marine armour in Vietnam was marked in the usual peacetime fashion; overall Forest Green with Chrome Yellow markings. In this case, some more personalised insignia have been added, including the card symbol and the eyes on the bulldozer blade.

E2: LVTH-6, Taiwanese Marine Division; Taiwan, 1983

The markings on this Taiwanese amtrac show American influences, both in the style of the Marine insignia, and in the peacetime US practice of painting grease nipples in red to make them easier to find for servicing.

F1: LVTP-7, Transport Company, Battaglione Marina 'San Marco'; Italy, 1984

Both the Army and Navy operated the LVT-7 in Italy. This vehicle from the San Marco Marine Battalion carries the battalion insignia – a San Marco lion on a red background –

Marines of the 5th Regiment, riding LVT-3 amtracs of the 1st Amphibian Tractor Battalion, pass through a North Korean village after the crossing of the Han River on 20 September 1950. The unmodified LVT-3 Bushmaster and the improved LVT-3C amtrac were both used in Korea. (US Army)

as well as the Navy's anchor symbol, and the Italian national colours on the hull front.

F2: LVTP-7, Argentine 1st Amphibious Vehicle Battalion; Falklands, April 1982

The LVTP-7s of this unit spearheaded the Argentinian attack on the Falkland Islands in 1982. The vehicles were finished in overall Forest Green with the vehicle number in yellow, the Marine anchor insignia in white, and the national flag carried above it.

G1: LVTP-7, US Marine 2nd Amphibious Assault Company; Grenada, 26 October 1983

Marine amtracs used in the Grenada fighting were plainly marked. The camouflage is a direct adoption of the US Army MERDC scheme, in this case with Field Drab and Forest Green as the primary colours, and Sand and Black as the subsidiary colours. The only insignia are the black vehicle markings.

The LVTP-5A1 was the standard troop carrying version of the LVT-5 series. The vulnerability of the LVTP-5A1 to land mines due to the location of its petrol tanks led most Marine infantry to ride outside the vehicle during fighting in Vietnam. This LVTP-5A1 carries Marines of the 4th Regiment during the fighting around Cua Viet and Dong Ha on 30 May 1968. (USMC)

G2: LVTP-7, US Marine 6th Amphibious Brigade; Italy, 1985

This Marine amtrac taking part in NATO exercises in Italy is finished much the same as the vehicle above, but has had the brighter Earth Yellow substituted as a subsidiary colour instead of the paler Sand. The black 'Pack Rat' cartoon is definitely unofficial, and this style of marking is very uncommon in the Marine Corps today.

COMPANION SERIES FROM OSPREY

CAMPAIGN
Concise, authoritative accounts of history's decisive military encounters. Each 96-page book contains over 90 illustrations including maps, orders of battle, colour plates, and three-dimensional battle maps.

ELITE
Detailed information on the uniforms and insignia of the world's most famous military forces. Each 64-page book contains some 50 photographs and diagrams, and 12 pages of full-colour artwork.

MEN-AT-ARMS
An unrivalled source of information on the uniforms and insignia of fighting units throughout history. Each 48-page book includes some 40 photographs and diagrams, and eight pages of full-colour artwork.

WARRIOR
Definitive analysis of the armour, weapons, tactics and motivation of the fighting men of history. Each 64-page book contains cutaways and exploded artwork of the warrior's weapons and armour.

ORDER OF BATTLE
The most detailed information ever published on the units which fought history's great battles. Each 96-page book contains comprehensive organisation diagrams supported by ultra-detailed colour maps. Each title also includes a large fold-out base map.

AIRCRAFT OF THE ACES
Focuses exclusively on the elite pilots of major air campaigns, and includes unique interviews with surviving aces sourced specifically for each volume. Each 96-page volume contains up to 40 specially commissioned artworks, unit listings, new scale plans and the best archival photography available.

COMBAT AIRCRAFT
Technical information from the world's leading aviation writers on the aircraft types flown. Each 96-page volume contains up to 40 specially commissioned artworks, unit listings, new scale plans and the best archival photography available.